CW00381144

SCHALK'S LITTLE BOOK FOR BROTHERS

Essential principles to understanding brotherhood.

Schalk Holloway

ISBN FOR PRINT EDITION: 9798364103611
Imprint: Independently Published

Cover design by: Schalk Willem Holloway

Dedicated to all of those that deeply desire the bonds of true brotherhood.

May you not just find good brothers, but may you become one as well.

INTRODUCTION

For many of us, the concept of brotherhood was entrenched (pun intended) in the literal and proverbial trenches.

Whether on the streets, in the military or other teams, or through the navigation of large societal chaos or deep personal adversity, a relationship was tested by fire and found to be gold: men, or women, were brought together, almost as if destined or divinely appointed, to face life, death, and all the tragic adversity in between, together.

However, using this as our point of departure, there are two sides of this coin that need to be brought to the foreground: first, some of us have stared death in the eyes, together, with no other option than to depend on one another; but second, some of us have never faced true life threatening or altering adversity at all, and so have never been forced to forge the bonds that this book will address.

We might say that the two dynamics above show the ends of a spectrum: on one side is a history that required that we might need to take life, or possibly give our own lives, to protect our brothers; on the other side is a history of such disconnect, or comfort, or maybe such safety and abundance, that we have never truly discovered, and much less understood, the divine necessity and blessing of being surrounded by true brothers.

And so the word is complex: for some it means I've killed for you, or I've almost been killed for you, and I'll do it again; for others it stands almost next to nothing, an empty term, meaning no more than 'hey, you'.

For many of us on the killing side of the spectrum, we use the term less and in a very specific manner. As such, we loath it when those on the comfort side of the spectrum call us, or anyone else for that matter, brother. Whether we say it or not, we are all thinking two things: one, you are not my brother; and two, you have no idea what you're talking about.

On the comfort side of the spectrum, and understandably so, some might label us as extreme, or as being unnecessarily difficult or exclusionary.

What compounds this complexity is the fact that some of us have transitioned out of the life, or the teams, or the times of adversity, which essentially means we are now playing life by a different set of rules. We're not that person anymore, or we've left that environment, or we might have found something else to live for or that's now a primary responsibility, like wives and children, and that's okay as well. But what then? Does, and how does, that redefine the parameters for being brothers?

This Little Book is an attempt to bring balance to these issues, to possibly help the pendulum to find a place of peace. If it's successful it might help some of us understand the word in a more healthy and balanced manner, and it might help some others, at the very least, to be more careful when they use it, but hopefully, to know that when they do use it, that it should actually mean something.

More than this, for myself, and coming from a Christian background, I fully believe that all of humanity should be treating each other as brothers, and especially so the church (of which Christ is the firstborn). But, unfortunately, as a church we frequently and sadly call others brother, while still lacking basic understanding of what the word truly means.

In this way, as we discover what it means to be a brother, we might also discover how we might treat others and, just maybe, as we start to actually treat certain individuals as true brothers, it might offer us a goal to aim for, a roadmap to navigate with, when it comes to developing others into better 'brother material', if I may.

The sad part, however, is that even if you had to treat every person you encounter in this manner, few will reciprocate. How you navigate this dilemma is extremely personal, but I will say the following concerning the matter: love all, but trust carefully, for there might come a day when you need to rely on someone, only to find them lacking the right stuff.

Conversely, if you are lucky enough to ever find a true brother, value him, guard him as real treasure, for he is a Godly gift and should be revered as such.

"A brother is born for adversity."

THE BOOK OF PROVERBS

CONTENTS

1. VALUES

Brothers Are Chosen On Values

The essential blessing, and very possible curse, is the fact that a brotherhood relationship is what we would call a yoked relationship. Meaning, I am yoked to my brothers. Visualise, for a moment, the image of two oxen yoked together, pulling the same load. They can pull significantly more weight precisely because they are yoked, but the presupposition is that they are working in concert, and that they are pulling in the same direction.

Now, on the one hand, it is the yoke that allows the energies of both oxen to be joined: it is the yoke that keeps them together and on the same path. However, if one of the oxen had to consistently try and pull in a different direction, or not even pull at all, this would create problems for the team.

When it comes to humans, it is our values which essentially determine the direction that we are pulling in. Our values set our bearing and our values will eventually determine where we end up in life. Some might call it a code, others an ethic, irrespective of semantics it is these principles by which we live that set our direction.

It stands to reason then, and experience easily proves it to be true, that when our values differ we will be pulling in different directions. This is especially evident in marriages where the partners haven't worked to align their values: they are constantly pulling against each other. Whether one partner is simply standing still, or whether they are pulling in marginally or completely different directions, it frustrates the team and lessens its effectivity and efficiency. In certain cases, it wears one or both partners out; in other cases, it pulls the team in a direction which it didn't actually want to go in, or maybe even shouldn't have gone in. Remove the yoke, and fast forward a couple of years into the future, and most probably the partners of this team would be in very different locations.

As such, you cannot truly be a brother to a man of differing values. Play it out logically: if you have made a commitment to honesty, but the other hasn't, eventually this will become a problem. If you have made a commitment to work hard and provide for your wife and children, and the other hasn't, how will this allow you to truly align the resources you are spending? With this I mean more than money: time, energy, and focus all come into play. If you are deeply convicted that you should be spending these resources on, say, your wife first, but the other party doesn't, it is evident that there is a misalignment of resource expenditure. Yoke yourself to this man and it'll wear you out, create frequent tension, or worse, pull you away from that which you know you should be focusing on.

Now, it may be that the yoke itself eventually creates a convergence of values; sometimes it is the patience of a brother that helps us grow and develop, that takes us off a certain path and shows us a different way. But isn't it exactly the consistency of that brother, his pure focus on what he believes to be right, that forces us and retrains us to a differing set of values? It is the tension created by him, by his uncompromising drive to remain true to his values, that pulls us alongside. Now imagine that same uncompromising drive in a person which have negatively differing values from our own, if we remain yoked to them they will retrain us, but not in a way that we deeply desire or have committed ourselves to.

So what then? Are we not to share life with those that differ from us? No, that's not the point at all. The point is that we should not yoke ourselves to them. To yoke yourself to someone is to allow them to have influence over you: we expose ourselves to this person, and open ourselves up to them, in such a way that they have a say in our decisions. When we consider a direction, or a certain decision, we allow their options as part of our options: this is what yoking does. Now when the values are shared, even just aspirationally so, that's good and can lead to positive growth and development; but when the values differ, it might very easily lead us down a path that we do not want to go.

Consider for a moment the joint venture between two new partners: the one is uncompromising in their ethical standards, the other fully believes that bribery is part and parcel of certain corporate or statutory environments. What do we do when the potential for bribery arrives within negotiations? How do we answer that question? Which direction do we go in? The differing values will at the very least create tension. However, repeat this scenario fifty times within three years, and suddenly there is massive opportunity to positively, or negatively influence, the other partner.

So some might ask but it isn't that good: shouldn't we aim to be a positive influence in others lives? To this I say yes, but without yoking yourselves to them, for who knows who will eventually capitulate?

Are you willing to expose your wife and children, your existing business or investment portfolio, your testimony before others, your eventual destination in life, are you willing to expose any or all of these to risk simply because you desire to be yoked to this other person? Or maybe you desire the benefit that that yoking might bring, in that case my question would be whether you are willing to risk any or all of those facets of your life for some potential or imagined benefit? How much would be enough, or what type of benefit would justify you risking those other and arguably very important components of your life?

This, essentially, is what we need to think about when it comes to choosing who we yoke ourselves to: what is my value system, or what would I have it be, and is this person that I'm calling brother, or aiming to call brother, aligned with those values? And if they aren't, how much am I willing to risk because of that? Because risk it is, and risk it will remain.

Brothers are chosen on values, and you don't call anyone

brother that doesn't share your values. A person that doesn't share your values is at best an associate, but better only an acquaintance. We can journey with this person, we can do business with them in the sense of buying, selling, or service acquisition or provision, we can learn from them or possibly glean inspiration from them, we can even socialise with them in certain limited fashions, but we can never yoke ourselves to them. We can never allow them to influence or determine our direction, and ultimately, our destination in life. We remain utterly responsible for those, and part of that responsibility is to ensure that we align ourselves with men that will pull in the direction we envision and desire for ourselves and our tribe.

This then is where we start when it comes to brothers: you need to make sure that your brothers share your values, and you need to do the work and take the time to discover those values before you yoke yourself to them.

2. GOALS

Brothers Purposefully Move Each Other Towards Their Individual Goals

Whereas the first principle, in a certain sense, might be concerned with the unintended consequences of a misalignment of values, this principles relates to the intended and purposeful attempts to assist our brothers in living out their values and reaching their destination.

However, this presupposes that your brother first understands you, and that you understand them. In understanding then we are aiming for a sober and accurate summation, one which stems from a deep insight into the type of men we are, and are striving to be, as well as the goals we feel led to pursue in life.

This step of understanding is important due to the issue of opinions and assumptions, of projecting our opinions and assumptions onto those around us.

If we are holding onto opinions and assumptions about each other, it means that we are not, nor will we ever be, able to give ourselves wholly to our brother's support and growth. We will justify our lack of involvement, our lack of care, our halting and superficial support, with the ideas that we entertain and uphold within our own minds.

Furthermore, irrespective of how a prospective brother might justify it, if they are projecting their opinions and assumptions onto you it indicates a probability of two things: arrogance; and possibly, hypocrisy.

Why arrogance, you might ask? Well, since we are talking

about brothers, let's assume that there's at least some healthy sharing of values. This should mean that you and your brother, deep down, already share the basic assumptions on life. When it comes to the pursuing of a certain goal, or maybe a direction in life, who then is to say that his opinions of your decisions is more accurate than your own?

Understandably, we want to listen to our brothers when it comes to serious, complex, or hot topics, but if we've listened, and after serious contemplation we are fully convinced of a course of action that isn't misaligned with our shared values, the question is begged: why don't they accept and support you in that decision? Is it because they are better than you? More intelligent? More logical or more intuitive? These are all steeped in arrogance. Again, I am contending that the work has been done: the thinking, the praying (if that's you), the pondering, the discussing, even the debate or healthy arguing, the work has been done and a person has decided on a course of action, it is here that the brother should let go of their arrogance and get behind you, especially so when the values still align.

And let's for a moment consider that you are unable to understand your brother's reasoning or motivations, for whatever reason, then why not support them in any case? Sometimes it's difficult for a person to accurately articulate or express themselves, other times we live by intuition or a sense of leading that we can't rationally explain, why does it have to make sense to you before you can fully commit to their course of action? If they are not venturing off the path, if they are not pursuing a direction contrary to the values you have established, why would you not fully support them? There is no other reason than 'it is your opinion that they should or shouldn't be doing this or that,' to which I say again, how arrogant are you to hold your opinion above the care of this person which you call a brother? No, this is not the way.

You might also ask, why hypocrisy? Because if any person is hiding, holding, or nurturing opinions regarding you and your life then it means that they are not being true: neither in their communication nor in their acceptance of who you truly are. It is very difficult to be a brother to a person like this: their opinions and their assumptions will always leak out, enter into the relationship, and create a toxic experience of tension. Meaning, you will intuit that they are holding the opinions and assumptions, and you will never truly feel safe, understood, or at peace within their company. Not truly. And so, the relationship, to a certain degree at least, becomes fake, and true brotherhood can never be fake.

What then to do if you are the guilty party? Repent of your arrogance, lay your opinions and assumptions aside, and try to understand your brother. Understand their thinking, understand their feeling, understand their desires and their goals, study them like you would study a complex subject - for aren't they worth it? And then when you understand them, align yourselves with their goals and aspirations and move the mountains to help them attain them.

Doesn't your heart resonate with that? Is that not what you yourself truly desire? To be encircled with strong men, that will lift your arms when you are tired, that will drag you over the finish line when you can't make it yourself, that will stand by you through thick and thin and see you reach all your lofty dreams and goals?

So, if it's you that's always holding onto opinions and assumptions on what you think your brother should and shouldn't be doing: just stop it.

If I call someone a brother, I need to understand them and I need to assist them in reaching their goals.

However, having said that, sometimes this will require a fight or two. Sometimes you will need to sit with a brother that's busy stepping off the path, and ask them what's going on here? You'll need to explain to them that you are seeing a worrying pattern emerge and you will need to ask them why it's there. This might need the application of force: that could mean you need to confront them, this confrontation might lead to conflict; it could also mean you need to take some other brothers with you and team up against him, treat it as an intervention; sometimes you'll have to plant your feet in his way or grab him by the nape and drag him kicking and screaming back onto the path, or even off the ledge.

This is necessary. We don't leave each other: we don't leave each other behind; we don't leave each other to drift off; and we definitely don't leave each other in the ditches or teetering on the edges. We do what is needed to ensure that we all stay on the path: this is what it means to help move one another towards our goals.

Life is tough. Sometimes it gets the better of us. Other times it tricks us and confuses us and drives us a little crazy. But when I truly understand my brother then I know where he's supposed to be headed, and I can clearly see when he's taken a wrong bearing. It is my duty as a brother to then do what's necessary to help him adjust that bearing, but this necessitates two things: first, that I fully understand and accept him; and second, that I'm willing to fight for him and his goals. It's not the one or the other, it's both. A brother does not impose their opinion, or limited insight, onto your goals.

3. PULLING WEIGHT

Brothers Pull Their Own Weight

A person that doesn't pull his own weight always falls into one of three categories: a free-loader, some American acquaintances recently taught me the word moocher and I am grateful to them for it, whether free-loader or moocher, both in my mind are technically cheats or scam-artists; the second is a lazy person, the one that is comfortable lying around procrastinating and wasting the opportunities they've been granted while the rest of us do the work; and lastly, the fool, that idiot that knows best but brings nothing to the table.

The essential problem with all three of these categories is that this person is comfortable being a burden to others, they are comfortable placing their interests above the interests of those around them. This essentially means that they deem themselves more important than you. How can we call such a person a brother? There can be no distinction in position or value when it comes to brothers: brothers are all equal, even if they are different.

This last proposition is very important to understand soberly: it might be that a brother is pulling their own weight even if they aren't making as much money as the other brothers. The ability to generate money is a complex capability with many variables: opportunity, experience, hard work, background, luck, gifting and wisdom, even something as simple as a stronger or lesser desire or interest in making any money at all, all of these factors come into play. It is natural, and human, and acceptable that some brothers make or earn more than others and I would encourage those that are doing better financially to guard their hearts in this aspect; never think because a brother earns less he is of less value or you are of more. This is arrogance of the worst kind.

The real question is what do the rest of their lives look like. Do they work hard? Do they do what life asks and requires from them? Do they treat their jobs, careers, hobbies, and pursuits with discipline and do they aim for mastery and excellence in execution? Do they attend to their wives and their children, or any significant other for that matter? Or are they comfortable sitting around at home, blaming this or that or the other for their lack of effort?

Furthermore, you might ask how they pull their weight within the brotherhood itself? Irrespective of whether they contribute money, do they contribute otherwise? Do they offer their skills or expertise when it comes to helping out? Do they offer their time and their hands and their ears and their firearms when those are needed?

There are many ways to contribute within a brotherhood, but the point is there is willing and eager contribution. They are pulling weight, and even more so, they are pulling some of the brothers' weight as well.

The item above brings us back to the previous principle: I need to understand my brother to be able to help pull his weight. Certain individuals will lay claim on their contribution, but their contribution isn't necessarily brother-focused. They only contribute what they feel like contributing, listen closely: they do not contribute what they are able to contribute, or what the brother truly needs, but only that which they feel like contributing; even though they are capable or more, they'll only contribute that which doesn't actually cost them anything.

But your brother might need something else: if he needs your time because he's struggling internally, don't just send him your prayers; if he needs financial support, and he's not a free-loader, or lazy, or a fool, meaning he's just truly and simply in need of help, then don't give him your ear, especially not when it's in your means to assist financially; if he needs your help when it comes to business or a connection, and you have the knowledge or the network, then don't just give him encouragement. Brothers pull each others weight, they don't just do what's comfortable or enjoyable to themselves.

A pattern should be emerging: if your brother is truly a brother, meaning he's not a moocher, or lazy, or a fool, and you can help them, then help them. It really is as simple as that.

Conversely, if he consistently displays one of those three dysfunctions, then he shouldn't be classified as a brother. He might have potential, or he might not, either way, he cannot be a brother for a brother is ready and able to pull his own as well as his brothers' weight.

Always remember, any person that'll place their interests above yours, outside of reasonable and healthy contexts, cannot be counted on. They are like drift sand, with an appearance of stability but offering no support when you walk into trouble; like a mirage that offers the hope of relief but turns up empty when you desperately need water; like a spare tyre full of holes. Why would you call such a person a brother? If you cannot depend on an individual, if you always have to wonder whether they've got your back or not, then you've yoked yourself to someone with differing values than your own.

To the free-loader, the lazy, and the fool, I'll say the following: get your act together. Who do you think you are to expect others to do for you what you won't do for yourself or for them? That's insanity. And while you're at it: how about you develop some self love and self respect? Is this what you want to be known for? A free-loader, a moocher, a lazy bum, a fool? Because others will label you as such. So get up off your ass and start pulling some weight: find strong men, those that seem to be good brother material, and start doing your part.

But remember, your part starts at home. It doesn't help you try and impress the brothers with everything you do for them but you're not pulling your weight at home, this is fake. And we can't be brothers with fake people. Furthermore, because it's fake, you'll only be able to hide it for so long before others pick up on it; before long they'll label you with a string of labels, the absolute worst of which is to deem you untrustworthy. Is this who you want to be?

So if you truly desire to have strong brothers, then you need to do your part. You need to be a man of means, capable to contribute and to bring value to the party. Not money, not always, but value. When you start walking in this others will see it, they will take note, and they will remember it. In this way you can start to nurture those deeply meaningful relationships that we call brotherhood.

4. FAMILY

Wives, Children And Other Brothers

All relationships fall somewhere within a scale of priorities and, although this remains personal to each individual, within the framework of this discussion it is given that our responsibilities to our wives and children precede our responsibilities to our brothers.

This stems from a deep conviction that the bond between life partners is based on a covenant of unity, which essentially means that the individuating lines between these partners blur when they enter this covenant: they become one person. It might take them a lifetime to develop that sense of oneness, and only a few ever fully realise it because it's immensely difficult work, but when I enter covenant with this other person they become a part of me and I of them.

This means that when my brother respects me, he respects my wife for she is an extension of me. When my brother commits to protect me, he commits to protect my wife for she is an extension of me. And lastly, when my brother commits to provide for me, he commits to provide for my wife because she is an extension of me. In this same manner children are extensions of that unity. It is therefore impossible to commit to a brother without committing to his wife and children, or what some might call his nuclear family.

In this same manner it becomes impossible for me to commit to my brother past my commitments to my nuclear family, for they are me. It would be a betrayal of self, and of those firstly entrusted to my guardianship and provision, should I choose my brothers before them.

True brothers, which share your values, will intrinsically understand and execute on this truth. They would not expect you to step out of unity with your wife, or to expose any of your nuclear family to unnecessary or unwarranted risk, because they understand that you will not arrive where you are needed whole and fully able to give yourself to the work. You will arrive fragmented, with divided heart and focus, and this could lead to serious harm or death.

What then? Should we never help a brother when the going gets dangerous? This is a question you would need to consider and discuss within the covenant relationship. If I may venture insight into the matter, I would say the following: the issue is of unity within the covenant. That means you don't move unless your partner's blessing is on the move. Some might feel that this holds us back, to which I say no, it protects us. The goal of an anchor is not to arbitrarily stop movement, but rather to protect the ship when the waters turn rough. As such, in a healthy covenant relationship, or marriage then, it is this unity in decision making that protects us and allows us to discern the correct paths when life gets dangerous or complex.

A brother then never says 'don't listen to your wife,' but instead asks 'what does your wife say about it?' Some might say, 'Well, that's never going to happen in my marriage,' to which I respond, 'barring exceptional circumstances, we all have the marriage that we build.' This I say without guile or condescension. It took myself and my wife many long years and many difficult conversations to reach this point of understanding, but we did the work. She now understands the type of man that I am: there are certain things I can't let go, if I did I wouldn't be the man that she loves. Subsequently, I have done many dangerous things, on many accounts through alternative channels and towards alternative goals, but our principle is what we believe protects us: I don't move unless we are in unity. This unity provides a twofold release: first, it allows me to know when it's safe to move; and second, we believe the shared ownership of the decision will provide relief and impetus for healing if I ever shouldn't return.

A brother understands this, he understands that our wives are not some curse that holds us back, but rather a blessing by which we can discern direction and by which we can either stay safe or better process grief.

This deep understanding of the worth of our wives should then allow us to cherish not only our own wives, but also the wives of our brothers. Coming from the Christian tradition I'm reminded of Paul telling Timothy that he should treat all other women as sisters. My brother's wife then is first and foremost intrinsically part of my brother, how I treat her is how I'm treating my brother, and then secondly she's my sister. This framework gives us a roadmap that I can use to guide me in treating with my brother's wife: I treat her like I treat him, and I treat her like I would treat my sister. I would not entertain, consider, attempt, or do anything with my brother's wife that I would not with my brother or with my own biological sister.

Conversely, I would not entertain any behaviour or advance from my brother's wife that falls outside of these bounds. Whether your relationship with your brother is developed enough to allow healthy discussion should you experience any untoward advances from his wife, can be a complex question to answer. It's dangerous to drive a 10t truck over a 5t bridge. What then? If you are not able to discuss it with your brother then it is your duty to remove yourself from any situations with the potential for untoward advances. Simply said: stay away from her, and especially from being alone with her. This is an act of respect and love for your brother: that you would take initiative to ensure that his wife remains protected even from herself.

In choosing our brothers we might also want to see how they treat their wives and their marriages. We are not looking for perfection, but we are looking for respect and for a striving towards unity. Does he make a habit of arbitrarily disrespecting and disregarding his wife? Well, you need to consider what that says about his values and how it aligns to your own. Furthermore, you need to consider that he probably doesn't understand deep or covenant relationships. And to this I ask: if he doesn't really understand the concept of a covenant relationship, then how will that translate into his ability to be a good brother?

You see, coming from a past on the streets, I used to confuse empty bravado, or a violent or unnecessarily risky approach to life, as an indication of good brother material. To this I say that it's easy to live a life of violence: do it long enough and it simply doesn't scare you anymore. It's also easy to die for someone, the important question was whether that death carried any true or eternal value?

What's difficult is to live a life that goes the distance, a life that pulls the weight: both the weight of the self and the nuclear family, as well as the weight of the brothers that remain standing when the dust has settled. When I was young I thought the truly difficult and noble test would be whether I would die for my brothers, and there were many instances where this was tested so I'm talking from experience, but now that I'm older I'm realising the truly noble and difficult thing is to actually live for my brothers; to be the type of man that loves and is able to support, that can share and help carry the load of those that I deeply care for. This is the true noble and difficult task of a brother.

What am I trying to say? It's simple, but very difficult: we best learn to love, support, carry, and share the load within a committed relationship with a significant other. Why? Because that's where we are truly tested, day in and day out, on the issues that pertain to the long game of life.

As such, for me, when I consider whether a man truly understands what it would mean to be a brother, I look at his marriage, or his relationship with his significant other, and I base much of my decision on that. Again, I'm not looking for perfection, I'm looking for healthy respect and for a striving towards unity. Why do I do this? Because I want brothers that deeply understand what it means to commit to someone, that can truly play the long game in the face of daily adversity; I don't want brothers that essentially only misuse me as place of safety, or that treat me as an escape because they aren't dealing with their issues at home. Obviously, both of these practices would be allowable as an exception, or within season, but not as a general rule of life. Good brother material handles their difficulties at home.

It is only the person that truly values, respects, and cares for himself that can truly value, respect, and care for others, including you: and the covenant relationship with a significant other is where we most clearly see this. How someone treats their significant other, is how they actually treat themselves, and, furthermore, is how they will eventually come to treat you if a difference in values remain.

Mark my words: unless you capitulate to the differing values, which, best case scenario, means that you start to accept and become silent about your brother's mistreatment of their significant other or children, or, at worst, means that you also start to disrespect and disregard your own significant other, the relationship that you think is a brotherhood won't make the distance. Speak up, and act up, concerning their bad treatment of their wives for long enough and they'll walk away. Become silent, and do nothing, and you have foregone your own integrity and will eventually capitulate.

This then is the unavoidable crisis when it comes to choosing brothers based on values: someone will need to change, and you will need to decide who that someone is going to be. Want a better marriage? Become brothers to men that treat their wives good. Want to maintain a healthy marriage? Don't yoke yourself to men that treat their wives bad.

5. HARD THINGS

Brothers Are Ready And Available To Do Hard Things

Brothers might occasionally need one another for some hard things, but those hard things should never unnecessarily compromise each others' families or interests. If I value and care for my brother's interests - whether his nuclear family, his wellness, his financial prosperity, or any other of his professional or personal interests - why would I unnecessarily jeopardise any of them? The caveat would be to return to the trenches mentioned in the Introduction: the streets, the teams, or possibly disaster or societal breakdown, where we are confronted with danger and risk in a more frequent and tangible manner. But, barring those, we should not intentionally or irresponsibly create unnecessary risk or danger for our brothers or their interests.

Interestingly enough, this principle is well understood by seasoned brothers. Frequently it's the young bucks that create problems in the life: still wanting to prove themselves, or possibly enamoured or emboldened by their brotherhood, they'll step out of line, create complications, and/or pick fights where it isn't needed. The old boys will instinctively avoid these where possible, risk and danger that is, but usually when they do flip the switch you want to be far away. In this sense, it's sometimes required to discipline the youngsters, to use whichever methods are necessary to reign them in and to get them to sober up and mature.

Furthermore, a brother should be careful about putting a brother in a position where they would need to go against their conscience. This shouldn't be an issue when the value systems are aligned but, if there is a conflict of conscience, it could and should be used as an impetus to ponder and/or discuss which differences in values are being highlighted and what to do about it. These discussions should be, and hopefully will be, completed before the day of testing comes.

To the crowd that wants to say, 'No, a brother should help regardless of conscience,' I say no. If I truly respect my brother, if I understand them and want to assist them in reaching their goals, then I would not expect something from them that misaligns with what they are trying to build. This is selfish and doesn't display true care for my brother. It is the mindset of a taker and not a giver.

This is especially important when it comes to expecting your brother to break unity with their significant other: again, you will end up with half a team member, someone who's focus and attention is divided by their conscience. The solution here is quite simple: if the person doesn't align with your values, whether they are expecting things from you that you aren't comfortable doing, or whether you require things from them that they aren't comfortable doing, simply step away. Reclassify them: remove them from the brother label and bump them to associate or acquaintance.

All of that said, some of us still live and function in environments that contain risk and danger. Context is important when it comes to this principle. For example, you might not live in a war zone, or on the streets, but you might live in a country that's ridden with violent crime. In South Africa, where I come from, there is constant risk of aggravated robbery: carjackings, home invasions, and muggings are part and parcel of living here. So what to do then if my wife, or a child, or some other dependant becomes a target or a victim of violent crime and I can't respond? Who would you call? And who would you prefer to depend on in a situation like this? The answer is obvious: someone that's trained and preferably also experienced; not just willing but also very much able to step in and do what needs to be done to get your family to safety. If a person is not able to do this, can you really call them a brother?

Some might say but that's unfair: not everyone is wired in that way. To which I say no. It has nothing to do with wiring, it has to do with responsibility. If you live or function within an environment with much risk and high probabilities of violence or other forms of danger then you need to make yourself adept at dealing with the potential issues. It might not be everyone's calling to become a first responder, daily entering into those environments, but it should be everyone's responsibility to be able to when needed and called upon. Let's forget about the issue of brotherhood for a moment: what about the self, or the nuclear family? Are neither of those valuable enough to skill up for? If not, if you won't even prepare yourself to protect your own wife and children, how can I trust you to protect me or mine?

And in any case, preparation comes on a spectrum: not all of us need to be fighters. There's a world of events that lead up to a critical incident, and there's always fallout that needs to be dealt with afterwards. This opens the door to things like Wilderness or Urban Survival, Escape and Evasion, Negotiation Skills, Driving and Advanced or Defensive Driving Skills, First Aid and Trauma Care, Places of Safety, even Counselling and Debriefing Skills: all of these are hard things to do. So no, everyone doesn't have to be a fighter, but everyone can pull some of the weight.

For me, personally, I find it hard to call someone brother if they aren't willing and able to offer this type of support. Acquaintance? Sure. Associate? Possibly, depending on the context. Brother? No.

If you might indulge me to digress, purely to touch on a pet peeve: stop saying I'll do this or that for you when it can't be tested. I say this especially in the light of today's social media environment where everyone wants to be seen and noticed. Making commitments, whether publicly or not, that cannot be lived out is not a ticket to brotherhood. Don't tell me you'll stand by my side in this or that manner, if you can't actually do it. It sounds all noble and nice but the reality is how would we know? It can't be tested, so better not to make the claim.

Even more so, if you haven't been tested when it comes to violence or other hard things you should rather keep your mouth shut completely. I've had men, not 'brothers' from that day onwards, run out on me while I'm getting my head kicked in on a pavement. You don't know how you'll respond when the day comes until the day comes. So work hard, train hard, prepare yourself, and then humbly pray and trust that when the day of testing comes, that you'll pass. Making a noise on social media only earns you derision from the men that have actually been there.

All of what I've said thus far was an attempt to bring balance, but now let us take it a step further: whereas all brothers should be able to do some hard things, you also need a few that are extremely dangerous. Very important: I'm not proposing gratuitously violent men, I'm proposing dangerous but disciplined men. A gratuitously violent man will create problems for themselves and for you, they will also assault and damage where it isn't needed, and this isn't honourable. And, in any case, those of us that have been around for a while know that it's usually easy to win a fight where you stack the deck and assault someone with surprise and overwhelming force. This isn't necessarily apt or honourable, so don't be fooled by it. Rather, find dangerous men, by nature and by training and by experience, that have a code, men that are willing and able to protect theirs, yours, and those that need it: meaning the truly weak, innocent, and vulnerable. And aim to be like that yourself. And then trust and serve and work hard so that you might become brothers with such men.

Let me end: just like free-loaders, lazy bums, and fools can't be brothers, those that are weak can never truly be a brother, because how can you depend on them when the day comes? Weakness is a state of mind, a posture of spirit, and it is something that can be untrained. Someone that's willing to forego doing the hard things, is someone that doesn't take up their responsibilities to care and to protect in the ways that the context demands. In this same manner cowards can't be brothers either, for again, how can you depend on them when the day comes? Cowardice, as well, has to do with training the will, the mind, and the body. There are exceptional cases where a human being is so traumatised that no effort or time will bring them back to a place of strength but, for the most part, it can be amended with hard work.

What then? Do we shun the weak and the cowardly? No, not at all. We care for them and we protect them, supporting and strengthening them where we can. But we can't depend on them, and this, unfortunately, means that they can't be our brothers.

6. PROVISION

Brothers Make Sure That Everyone Has Enough

There is a Biblical principle that's central to this theme: Paul states that at times, some might have abundance and some need, and at other times, that those positions might be reversed. I might be doing well today and my brother might be struggling, but tomorrow my brother might be doing well and I might be struggling. Paul's admonishment is that in all seasons we should be supplying to each other's needs, the one that has more should be giving to the one that has less. He sees this as so fundamental that he even calls it a point of fairness: it is fair that I supply to your need today because it's a given that you'll have to supply to me when I'm in need. There's no argument concerning whether we should supply to each other's need, it's a given that we would.

There are some, usually those that are currently in abundance, that might be resistant to this idea. It can be that they've given wrongly or unwisely in the past and, as such, have built up resentment concerning the issue. To them I say the following: the principles will safeguard you. 'What are the principles?' You might ask. Well, we've already discussed them: first, care for brothers, if you have chosen them according to this treatment then they won't be free-loaders, lazy bums, or fools; second, supply to their needs, especially things like shelter, food, and other essentials; third, contribute from a place of abundance, with this I don't mean that it shouldn't cost you anything. The principle is really quite simple: if you currently have more than your brother then it means that you are in a position of abundance and that you have enough to contribute.

In keeping with the rest of the book, the obvious consideration would be that you remain in unity with your significant other and that you only very carefully supply at cost to your nuclear family. Very practically: don't take the food from your child's mouth, take it from your own.

There are two categories of persons that struggle immensely with this concept: those that have always had enough, for they have no concept of what it means to lack even the basic necessities of life and, as such, struggle with empathy; and those that have struggled but have forgotten where they came from. Whether due to their success, or the insecure guarding of what they've accumulated, they've conveniently forgotten that there's no such thing as a self made man and that they themselves received different types of assistance throughout their own lives.

Brothers, however, make sure that everyone has enough. Their ears are on the ground, they are watching each other keenly, and when they note a real and valid need they are quick to step in and to assist where and how they are able to.

Why do they do this? For two reasons: first, they understand that they are their brother's keeper, they don't "have" to care for their brother, they are "entrusted with" and "may" care for their brother, they see it as a privilege and not a burden; and second, they are instinctively, even if subconsciously, aware of Paul's principle of fairness, for who knows what the future holds? It is ever and only the hubris of financial success, a very one dimensional type of success if I may add, that supposes that security is a given. It says, 'Look at me and what I've amassed, I'm safe and I shall never need to worry again.' But, honestly, what do we know about what's to come? And how arrogant would we be in any case to assume that we have full knowledge or control over the future. As such, it is a very human aspect to provide for the tribe, because one day the tribe might need to provide for me. And in this sense, the nuclear family is the first tribe and the brotherhood the second. I am sowing into another's field in the expectation that one day they'll sow into mine.

Conversely, a person that's always reliant on handouts can't be a brother; hand ups are good, a hand forward even better, but never constant handouts. Persons that require constant handouts may be children, or disciples, or prospects, or mentees, or any other form of dependant, but they are not brother material. Remember, a brother is able to pull their own weight and takes responsibility not to be a burden on the brotherhood.

However, it's important to note this topic of handouts extends to what we might call a mindset. It is the person that's in a mindset of wanting or requiring constant handouts that needs to be carefully considered before being made a brother. A brother has a mindset of doing the work, but they might find themselves in need or lacking the ability to cover certain costs or essentials. These are two different persons and they need to be considered differently.

Furthermore, let's not quibble about things that are irrelevant: if you know your brother's struggling but you really feel like going out or doing something fun then simply pick up his tab; if it's within your means, it'll be safe to keep on paying for him as a true brother will return the favour in some other way. Conversely, if neither of you can afford to do something, then discuss it and choose to do something that won't put either of you under pressure.

Again, if you have chosen well, your brother might be providing much value of the type that surpasses the cost of beer or dinner. So stop evaluating life from a perspective of money, it's foolish and it will rob you of meaningful times with good men. Rather, if you are brothers, simply discuss matters: is there money for something, who can contribute what, and then pick something that's affordable and go and have a good time. Because really, if you make it to an old age and you put your head down that final time, and you're still lucid, it's not the money that'll come to mind: it'll be the camaraderie, and the laughing, and the embraces, and the deep and meaningful conversations. This is what you are spending on, not the beer and the food.

To summarise then, a brother never looks away. Sometimes they don't even ask the question, 'What do you need?' Because they are actively engaged, they step in and they provide. They are willing to open their own cupboards and split the contents in half, and they are willing to open their safe and count out what's needed; what they have is yours and likewise, what you have should be theirs. It would be a disgrace if a brother was left at home, or left behind, when there were means to provide what they were lacking.

That said, if you are the one that's being left at home, or left behind, then you need to soberly evaluate the reasons, and you need to be very honest with yourself. If you are a free-loader, a lazy bum, a fool, or one of those which has a mindset of constantly receiving handouts, then you need to shape up. If you aren't pulling any weight no-one is obligated to stick around with you. Furthermore, if you have become comfortable within this mindset I, personally, would struggle to see you as an honourable man. So fix it.

Conversely, if you know that you aren't any of those, that you are an honest man and that you are doing the work, but it's simply that you don't make as much as the others, and they are leaving you at home or behind when it is within their means to take you along, then you need to let go of them. Stop seeking their attention or acceptance because they aren't worthy of yours.

Good brother material will look past the surface, they will see and acknowledge you for the man you are, and if they don't then stop pursuing the relationship. But again, you need to be very honest with yourself: don't try and justify your own bad character and/or lack of effort by shaming other hardworking men. Be sober about it, and let the answers inspire you to movement and growth.

7. SEASONS

Brothers And Seasons

Many of us feel that brothers are supposed to be for life, but the reality is that some might take a different path and others may pass away.

In terms of those who take a different path, it usually relates to either a process of growth, or a serious incident of conflict. Both of these, however, can usually be traced back to the question of values; a divergence of paths was brought forth by a commitment to different bearings.

This isn't always bad: I've made decisions myself to separate from men that I once thought of as brothers.

Currently, at 41 years of age, I can sincerely say that there are only three men that I have stepped away from and that I probably won't ever attempt to reconcile with. I wouldn't say reconcilement is impossible, but it would be highly improbable. Why? Because all three men, even though two were close business associates and one even a pastor, were caught lying about us behind our backs. Furthermore, it wasn't "innocent" little white lies, if lies can ever be innocent, little, or white for that matter, it was intentional and malicious lies purposed to cause myself and my house harm. In a sense, betrayal of a very dubious kind.

These men have shown themselves to be untrustworthy and, unless there's a long and consistent attempt of trying to rebuild that trust from they're side, it would be very difficult for me to ever relabel them as trustworthy, and nigh on impossible for me to ever call them brother again. In cases like these I feel comfortable stepping away, even though it might hurt tremendously: and you should feel comfortable doing so as well. Anyone willing to betray you isn't worth your time or energy. There's Biblical mandate to reoffer them your trust, but the examples are clear: they have to come to the party in a very significant way.

Not to try and sound too apocalyptic, but woe betide you if you were the one that betrayed a brother. There's not a lot to say concerning this side of that coin: if you've ever done that, you learn from it and you never, never do it again.

On the other hand, some of us have lost brothers to the life, or in armed conflict, or to the crises and tragedy of life: a devastating blow that can at most be numbed but never not be deeply felt.

Here's the thing: irrespective of how we might lose a brother, sometimes we do lose them. And the more sudden and complete, the more difficult it is to process the loss. Why? Because we don't always understand or embrace the process of grief that accompanies loss. We shun the emotions. Whether due to being emotionally disconnected, being afraid of experiencing the hurt and the pain, or simply not having the time to experience the emotions right now, we shove them aside and try to keep them in a box. The problem with this is that they'll eventually climb out of the box, and we might not like how they climb out when they do.

Losing a brother, for whatever reason, is a hurtful life-event. It causes a rollercoaster of emotions and it requires large amounts of time and attention to process well and in a healthy manner. We need to attend to this if we want to avoid coming apart later in life.

Furthermore, when we don't attend to the grief, we can never fully move forward in life. In therapeutic circles there are diagnoses of what's called Delayed and/or Complicated Grief. Without getting too technical or digressing: they mean exactly what their names imply. Grief will not go away unless experienced and processed. When we don't grieve we get stuck: stuck in the past, stuck to that experience, and stuck to the person that we're grieving about.

For some it might feel like a very final betrayal to say that we need to move forward, but we do need to move forward. If we don't we'll eventually medicate, or worse, ourselves out of the game of life.

To be successful at the long game of life, and to remain able to do the very difficult and noble work of staying available to the brothers that are still at our sides, we need to find ways of letting go of the past and pressing forward into the future. If we want to remain true to our brothers of the day, our brothers alive, we need to have space for them in our hearts and in our minds. However, when our hearts and our minds are dominated by our brothers past, this unfortunately becomes impossible. The brother that has left is tangibly taking up the space of the brother that's still around. And so, to honour our brothers alive we need to let go of our brothers past.

But what am I saying, then? Aren't we dishonouring our brothers past if we let them go? To answer that we need to consider what it means to honour someone, or more accurately, to live a life that honours someone. This is readily definable: to live a life that honours someone is to live a life that they would be proud of. So I remember my brothers past, and I strive to live a life that they would have been proud of, but I don't let them take up space, for that space is precious and limited and there are good men that need it today. This is the way that I would venture that your brother past would have it in any case. If he was a true brother, he would want the best for you in every season of your life.

So we have to grieve, we have to remember, we have to bring honour, but we also need to move on and resist the temptation to stay stuck in the past.

Our brothers alive need every part of us, not just the parts that were left after the blow of loss.

8. CONCLUSION

Conclusion

To some it might be evident that I haven't spoken overtly about the idea of respectful behaviour. I know the topic's quite popular these days: all the little memes and motivational messages and posts about giving and receiving respect and whatnot, but among true brother material this is a non-issue, a given. If someone isn't being respectful, it's intrinsically difficult to see them as respectable, very little discussion on the matter is actually required.

Also, this is very easy to treat with: give a person at least one chance, meaning state your expectation and/or boundary clearly and accurately, if they don't acquiesce then don't consider them. Again: disciple, or mentee, or prospect maybe, but not a brother. And in any case, life is too short to waste on fools, so don't.

Let me end with this: the essential defining characteristic of relationships are what we would call "shared experiences". Any relationship is the sum total of a string of shared experiences.

It's also one of the most challenging truths in today's digital society: I'm constantly looking for, and frequently struggling to find, ways of sharing experience with men that I've met on the digital landscape. And so, behind the scenes, I'm always trying to offer support or tackling little projects that might be of value to them. Why do I this? And why do I mention it? Not because I'm trying to impress the recipient (or you, the reader) with my effort, but because I sincerely desire an authentic relationship with the person on the other side. But relationships can only be made up of shared experience, so it's tricky.

To be honest, talk alone isn't enough, either. At some stage the talk has to move beyond mere words into the realm of value provision. Because if your talk and your actions don't provide any form of value, then there's no real shared experience. And so I try, consistently, to express gratitude, or to be involved, or to try and learn and understand about their lives, and where possible, to help and assist with things as and when the opportunity arises. Why? Because I desire their true friendship and possibly even their brotherhood. But this only comes with the type of effort that leads to shared experience.

You can't be a brother to someone you aren't sharing life with. Acquaintance? Sure. Associate, in some cases. Brother? Definitely not.

This also brings me full circle to the pet peeve that I mentioned earlier: be careful to call someone brother online if you can't figure out how to share experience with them, and if you are actually able to share experience but you don't make the effort to, then don't call them brother at all. Words alone, whether spoken or whether typed in posts, comments and messages, don't make brothers: effort and blood, hard work and sweat, understanding and tears, many hours and long years, these are the things that true relationships are built of.

So, if you can't find a way to share those with someone online, then simply don't call them brother, instead, keep focusing on finding and nurturing brotherhood relationships in your offline life. Go out and find men in your workplace, or in your church, look for them in your parks and your gyms and on your beaches, and if you're still hanging out in the pubs and the clubs then so be it: find them there, but make sure they share your values. I've said this many times and in many places: show me who you walk with and I'll know what type of man you are.

Always remember the essential characteristic of relationships: if there's no shared experience then it simply isn't real. If you want to be a brother to someone, you have to make time and effort for them: and if you really, really want it, it might even mean that initially all the time and effort has to come from your side.

My desire for everyone that reads this is simple: may you find good men to call brothers, strong, courageous and dangerous men, and may you give yourself to them as they give themselves to you. And if you can't find them, then start with yourself, become good brother material: look after your nuclear family, work hard and help pull the weight of those around you, care and provide to those that are in need, be willing and able to do the hard things, give your time and energy and expertise to invest in those around you. And then trust that someone will notice.

May you not only find brothers of worth, but more importantly, may you become one.

DID YOU ENJOY
THIS BOOK?

The best way to thank an author for writing a book you enjoyed is to leave an honest review! If you are reading on paper you can do so by heading back to the page you purchased this book from. Alternatively, select the link below to post your review of 'Schalk's Little Book for Brothers'.

Thank you so much for taking the time to let other readers know what you thought of my book!

(PS. I sincerely love photos of books - and photos of my own books all the more! :D If you have any feel free to share one with me on social media; I'll be sure to post it and then credit you!)

Click here to review.

FOLLOW SCHALK TO
KEEP UPDATED

facebook.com/schalkhollowayauthor

instagram.com/schalkhollowayauthor

amazon.com/author/schalkholloway

www.schalkholloway.com

Schalk is a South African author known for The Maul Book, Schalk's Little Book Series, and Die Groot Storie. Schalk started his career as novelist in 2022 after suffering and recovering from a serious injury. His first novels, the Brooklyn Saga, drew inspiration from the years that he ran interventions in that tiny Cape Town suburb.

Schalk's professional background lies in Christian ministry, combatives and firearms instruction, as well as tactical and intelligence based operations in select security and policing environments (references available upon request).

OTHER BOOKS BY SCHALK

(AS FOUND ON AMAZON)

NOVELS

The Brooklyn Saga:

Disciple's Fault
Brother's Request

SUBJECT LITERATURE

The Maul Book (co-authored with Gavin Coleman)

The Little Book Series:

Schalk's Little Book on Fundamentals (The Black Book)
Schalk's Little Book of Combative Principles (The White Book)
Schalk's Little Book for Brothers (The Red Book)

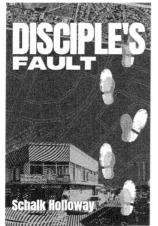

Disciple's Fault on Amazon

Frank Night is a lay minister that spends all his free time running interventions in at-risk communities. When the tiny community of Brooklyn, Cape Town, offers him two new cases, an unconventional stabbing leading to the death of a local boy, and a self-mutilating girl that disappears one Saturday night, he suddenly finds himself with much to do and manage.

A diagnosed neuro-divergent, his interactions with others are strained and complex at the best of times. But when the stress from these two interventions, as well as what seems like a neighbourhood that's set itself against him, starts to mount, he finally loses control. Just for an instant he becomes the man he used to be. Unfortunately for them, that single misstep places his wife firmly in the crosshairs of one of the local monsters.

REVIEW:

"Schalk's background gives him a huge edge when it comes to details and visualizations. The story is incredible and though written like a novel I get subtle hints that most of this book was written with experience. This is a great read and gives you a small slice of the pie in the combative world and life in Cape Town." - Loni Young

Brother's Request on Amazon

It's a couple of months after that disturbing night in Brooklyn. Frank and Didi have just started settling down but Brooklyn and the community's at it again: Jenny brings over a silent and highly detached friend, a new prostitute starts working their corner, and whereas Hamma's eventually finding his feet, certain interactions between him and the community has Frank concerned.

As if all of that isn't enough, even while Frank's trying to manage his neuro-divergence, he's also realising that he might slowly be losing control. Half the time he can't sleep due to nightmares and the other half is dominated by his recurring flashbacks. To complicate matters even further: a ghost from his past arrives in the neighbourhood.

A formidable man, and one that he used to call brother.

The Maul Book on Amazon

Did you know that the latest technology and research shows that the brain undergoes very specific changes in its functioning during a close combat incident? Whether training for self defence, law enforcement / military close combat procedures, or traditional martial arts and sports fighting - under certain conditions the brain will switch from one mode of functioning to another.

The Maul Book is the first book to delve into this research, and through extensive testing within different close combat environments, integrate this research into new and fresh training methodologies. The Maul book is a must for any practitioner from any martial arts, self defence, close combat or tactical environment, as well as for instructors serious about providing the best training developed and influenced through the latest research.

Here's what you will learn from The Maul Book:

• What the latest research teaches on the brain's functioning under certain conditions.

• Old brain models that have now been shown as defunct and obsolete.

• How the changes in brain function influences performance and decision making within highly dynamic environments.

• How to better identify and select targets within high speed and ever changing situations.

• Techniques, tactics and training methodologies that work WITH the brain and its different ways of functioning.

• How to apply this research into any martial art or close combat training system.

• The core knowledge base of The Maul as an example of how to integrate the research into an existing system.

REVIEWS:

"I could easily just state that this is one of the best books on knife combatives I have read, ever, and be done with it. But that would be a disservice to both the authors and to you, the reader… It is, quite simply, the best approach to realistic knife combatives written in years… I cannot give it a higher recommendation than this, read it, practice it, read it again, and keep working it. This is good stuff. I wish this book was out when I started in this arena." - Terry Trahan

"The Maul tells you why some things probably won't work and why you should reassess your own training to realign it with what is currently known about the human brain. This is the most important book on Defensive Edged Weapons to come out in years." - Don Rearic

Schalk's Little Book on Fundamentals on Amazon

Striking and take-downs are the two primary tools in the martial arts or combatives practitioners arsenal. However, when we do not understand the fundamentals behind these tools they inevitably degenerate - strikes become less and less powerful and takedowns are ineffective and easily resisted or countered.

In this Little Book:

• How all take-downs fundamentally work and how to fix take-downs that aren't effective.

• How you can perfect your own take-downs as well as identify which take-down to apply to an opponent and when.

• How to generate the maximal amount of force in your strikes.

• How to ensure that the force generated is actually applied to your opponent.

• How to stop the generated force from bleeding or dissipating before making contact with your opponent.

And herein lies the purpose of this little book on Fundamentals. It is little in the sense that it means to offer a concise, easy to study and easy to assimilate, treatment on the topic of Fundamentals. Its aim, with a laser like focus, is on educating both the practitioner and instructor with the Fundamentals pertaining specifically to combatives and martial arts. Its goal is to assist the reader to not only sharpen up, but rather to excel, in all aspects of their fighting career.

The "Schalk's Little Book Series" is a collection of concise treatments on certain martial arts and combative related themes and topics. All the books are just under 10 000 words in length and purposefully designed to be easily digested and referenced.

REVIEW:

"I've had the privilege of being instructed by Schalk and assisting him instruct others over the years. He is one of the few people who are natural born teachers and has a remarkable ability to assimilate information and deliver it in a concise and easy to understand way. Even complicated technical subjects. This is what the Little Book of Fundamentals does. For someone like me who comes from a very informal Combatives background, I've always felt my understanding of fundamentals is lacking. A book like this goes a long way to patching up that fundamental information and gives some practical guides to troubleshooting any issues you may be having with takedowns or striking. A handy thing to have." - Gavin Coleman, co-author of The Maul Book and owner at Ironside Edgeworks

Schalk's Little Book of Combative Principles on Amazon

Combatives, both in the sense of a set of techniques as well as a complete system, runs on very specific principles. These principles differ significantly from traditional martial arts and sport fighting systems. Most frequently combatives are applied within combat, law enforcement, security or self defense contexts. This means that the risk of severe injury or death is ever present. When we don't understand or incorporate true combative principles into our training we run the risk of losing within a context where losing can cost us our lives.

In this Little Book:

• The 3 main contextual considerations when it comes to combatives training and development.

• The importance of understanding your context and the factors that are influenced by context.

• Introduction to the Combative Triad.

• The core principles for successfully managing close combat incidents.

• Considerations on what needs to be included in training to successfully incorporate these principles.

The "Schalk's Little Book Series" is a collection of concise treatments on certain martial arts and combative related themes and topics. All the books are just under 10 000 words in length and purposefully designed to be easily digested and referenced.

REVIEW:

"Each time I read a new title by Schalk, I get happy, because good, useful information is about to get in the hands of people that need it. These "Little Books" are extremely valuable, and written in a very concise yet readable style. The newest one in your hands now, gives a very good overview of the training principles that really are universal, and important to successfully navigating the real world use of Combatives. There is no fluff between these covers, no padding of the lessons, just like Combatives, they are short, to the point, and if understood and trained, give you great bang for your buck. There is also plenty of room in this short book to work and wrestle with the lessons, to really make them yours, and apply them. I can't recommend this enough. Good, usable, concise, well presented, and accurate. This is a book you will keep going back to, as your eyes open, and your understanding grows." - Terry Trahan